I0463559

APPOWER:
A Guide to Mobile App Marketing Success 2014 Q4 Edition

By Carson Barker & Clif Haley

www.APPSPIRE.me

Copyright © 2014 APPSPIRE.me Publishing

Contents

Introduction

Welcome to the world of mobile apps and thank you for downloading our book. If you're reading this, you more than likely fall into one of these three categories:

- You have a mobile app (or apps) which you want more downloads, media coverage, or higher rankings for.
- You are about to launch a mobile app and are researching for the best methods to do so, or
- You are curious about the world of mobile apps and are wondering how they can be profitable.

Regardless of which of these categories fits your description, you'll find all the necessary information you need and more in here. Whether you're an app developer or just a creative mind with an interesting idea for an app, we'll show you step-by-step methods on how take your app from zero downloads per day to thousands, and how to go from ranking nowhere in the iTunes or Google Play stores to ranking #1.

How do we know this information? We've been in mobile app marketing since 2009, and we've learned what makes apps successful and what makes them fail.

We've had app owners come to use with an app that was nowhere to be found in the iTunes or Google Play store, and through our efforts, we pushed them to the top 3 in a matter of days. We've had clients that have had no press coverage or reviews, and we've got them featured on TechCrunch, Mashable, Huffington Post, and Fox Business News. Many of our clients stop calling us after one of our mobile app marketing campaigns because their app has become successful. That's fine with us. That's our job.

All of this being said, the road to the top is never easy. There are hundreds of apps being uploaded to iTunes and Google Play each week. Whatever type of app you have, there are more than likely dozens of others just like it. Climbing to the top takes innovation, determination, and thinking outside the box to figure out how your app can rise above the noise.

After we announced that we were writing this book, many of our colleagues, clients, and friends said, "Why are you giving away all of your secrets? Aren't you worried that it will hurt your business or empower your competitors?" In short, no. Knowing how to use a tool and being good at using it are two different things. If one of our readers were to implement every strategy in this book, they would need to hire an entire team to do it. And they could hire some great employees with little or no experience, or they could hire professionals, like us.

Listed in this book are the tools and strategies to make a successful app, but the real secret is conjuring up innovative ideas for press releases, creative link bait, ads, real world marketing, brand identity, social media campaigns, compelling designs and so forth. An engine powers a car, but ingenuity and know-how tells it where to go. The creative basis of your campaign is up to you and your team.

Depending on your app and the market, you might not have to use every single strategy listed in this book. You might already have some decent press coverage; you just want to learn how to run an ad campaign. Or, you might already have a campaign going, but you want to be featured in major media sites or learn how to effectively run a successful social media campaign. Whatever your situation is, you can pick and choose which sections in this book work the best for you.

Testimonials

 *"Carson definitely knows what he is doing. We're seeing an 80-90% increase in downloads as a result of APPSPIRE.me1and1's efforts."*- Project Capture

 *"APPSPIRE.me's got a record including more featured apps than I can count, and Carson's the brains behind making apps into hits." - Rocksauce Studios*

 *"Their knowledge on the mobile app marketing segment is unparalleled. -Idea2Appstore*

 *"These packages have made a HUGE difference in introducing my app to the right app users and I'm so pleased with the results. - Princessy Cupcakes*

 *"APPSPIRE.me's services are a necessity for any app's success."- Blue Whale Apps*

Designing Your App

Once you've got your app idea, which is usually where most people start, it's time to start looking for a developer. App developers nowadays are like web developers: they're all over the place. You can find any type of app developer from a one-man-job working out of his garage, to a large company working out of a skyscraper in NYC. The point of all this is to find the right one for you. Here's a checklist to go over to help you find the perfect developer for your app.

1. **Find a developer that has made apps like yours.**
   - This is imperative. If you have a game app, find a developer that has created games. If you have a social media app, find a developer that has created social media apps. If the developer already has experience in the field, the time and process of creating the app will be much more streamlined.
2. **Get a contract signed with a set amount of revisions.**
   - More than likely you are not going to be satisfied with the first draft of your app, so you need to make sure that your contract details a finite amount of revisions, hard dates on completion, and so forth.
3. **Expect to pay more that you expect.**
   - Don't short change your app because development went over your expected budget. App development is one area that you need to have perfect. If the app development fails, the whole business fails.

Great vs. Terrible Design

There is no gray area for a successfully designed app. App designs are either perfect, or they fail. Your app needs to look, feel, and function perfectly to beat the competition. Key points that you need to focus on are:

- Color palette,
- Structure, font choice,
- Layout, functionality,
- Ease of use,
- Simplicity,
- Framework, and more.

Get these preliminary aspects settled on early on to ensure a great app design.

Iconography

The icon for your app is your business card, and the first portal for users to go through in order to download your app. We cannot stress the importance of a well-designed icon. Think of the most successful apps available today: Twitter, Instagram, Angry Birds – just reading the names of these apps puts the image of their icon in your head.

Your icon should be as simple as possible, and represent your app and brand without question. Instagram is a camera, Facebook is the letters F, Twitter is a bird, think about what your app does and what basic image can represent it the best.

Also, bear in mind that your app icon is going to be really small on someone's phone, so details should be big and bold, not tiny and elaborate.

How powerful is your app icon? Can you imagine it on a t-shirt? A coffee mug? As a tattoo? If not, go back to the drawing board and streamline it some more.

Your icon colors and font should match what is in the app design for consistency. Pro-tip: Stay away from using commonly used app icon colors, like blue. Blue is the most widely used app icon color, every app from Facebook to Twitter uses it. If your app icon matches several other popular app icons, then it will be harder to find on the mobile device because it will be camouflage. This reduces the number of times your app is used and ultimately, decreases your user engagement and ROI.

Cover these bases when creating your app icon. It should be a powerful branding image that people only need to see a few times to get stuck in their heads. When you mention your app's name to someone, they should automatically picture the icon in their head.

ASO
(App Store Optimization)

ASO is an imperative part of a successful app. Similar to SEO, ASO is the process of optimizing your app so that it ranks accordingly in the app store, and converts users to download it. It's an expansive process that includes Keywords, App Description, Screenshots and more.

Keywords

Keywords are words or terms that users would search for that relate to your app. For instance, if you had a photo-sharing app, "social photo" might be a key term that you would use. Or if you had a GPS map app, "GPS" and "direction" might be keywords that you'd use. Discovering which keywords are best suited for your app, and rank the highest, is an encompassing task, but you can start in the right direction by searching key terms in Google Keyword Planner, and investigating what keywords your competitors are using.

Once you have your keywords settled upon, you can implement them in your app's description. In iTunes, there's a section where you can put the keywords alone to ensure better ranking results. Google Play doesn't have this option, so a new trend for Android apps is to *tastefully* put them in the app's title. An example would be "Tripbook: Photo Travel Scrapbook" or "Mapquest: Maps, GPS, and Traffic." Adding the keywords in your Google Play app description helps improve search results.

App Description

App description optimization is a major functionality of ASO as well. Your app description should be as short as possible, to the point, and broken up into short paragraphs or stand-alone sentences. The very first sentence should be your tagline; the rest should be reverse-pyramid style writing. Also, if you have any impressive quotes from notable personnel, or impressive figures like "Rated Top 10 Apps of 2014 by TechCrunch," include these in quotes at the top as well. Anything to grab attention and keep users reading, but too much info will drive users away. Your app description is a sales pitch, not an instruction manual.

Screenshots

Both iTunes and Google Play let you add screenshots of your app to further entice users and describe your app. Your first screenshot should be your homepage, because it is simple, and effective for branding. Your next screenshots should be pics of the app in action, significant pics that make your app standout from others, and more.

Establishing a Presence on the Internet

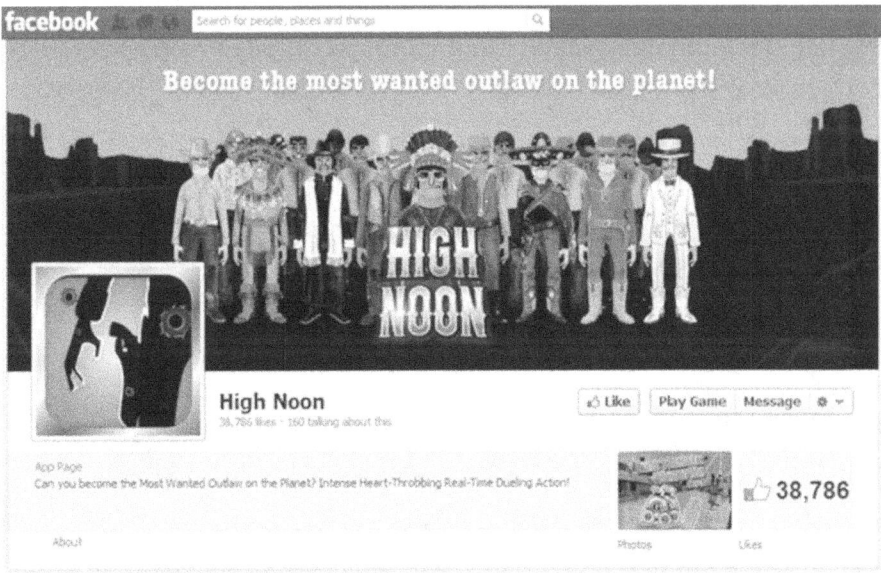

Facebook fan page for the popular game app High Noon.

Although people will be downloading and installing your app from their respective app marketplaces – the iTunes App Store or Google Play – you should still establish a presence on the web at large. By getting information about your app online, you are able to reach more potential customers, not just the people who happen to be shopping in the app market or who might see an in-app ad that you've paid for. You can then build awareness of your app in search engines and social media networks where millions of people are "hanging out" all the time.

Having a web presence provides several ways that you can maintain an open line of communication with your current customers, which is a great way to make sure they will also be your future customers. A vibrant web presence full of regular news about your current apps and upcoming new releases keeps customers engaged in your brand. You can have people sign up for email newsletters, or follow you on social networking websites like Facebook and Twitter so that you can market directly to them with new updates and app launches.

Here are all the ways that you can leverage the power of the Internet to build a strong presence for your app. Use all of these together to ensure optimal exposure and discovery for your app.

Build a Website

Building a website for your app is incredibly beneficial, whether it is for your app, specifically, or for your overall app development business. A website serves as an official home base on the web for your app and provides a way for people to find your app outside of app market places, such as in web search engines. Your website is the professional face of your app where people can learn more about it, your company (or you) and related information.

If your website is the professional face of your app on the web, then it is important that your website looks professional. Your website should look great and function well. It should not look like it was built by someone who has zero web design skills. Luckily, these days it is very simple for almost anyone to set up a great looking website with very little knowledge of web design. Steps to setting up your website can be as simple as:

1. Register a domain name. Your domain name can either be the name of your app, or a keyword very closely related to what your app does. For instance, let's say your app generates virtual widgets and is called Widget Master. Your domain might be widgetmaster.com or it might be virtualwidgets.com or even virtualwidgetapp.com. Registering a domain name based on a keyword can help your website get found in search engines. More on this later.
2. Purchase a web hosting account and install WordPress. There are tons of web hosting providers on the web, many of them perfectly suited to your needs. Just make sure that the hosting provider you choose does, indeed, provide an install of WordPress.
3. Install an attractive WordPress theme. WordPress comes with lots of free themes that can give your website a professional appearance, but if you really want to have the best looking website possible, you should invest in a professionally designed theme. WordPress themes are very affordable and often times for a small additional fee, the designer will install it for you.

 Because of its ease of use, making it a great option for both experienced and beginner web designers, the popularity of WordPress continues to skyrocket. Web trends analyst website BuiltWith.com reports that, in their database

alone, there are over 8,000,000 million websites currently using WordPress (http://trends.builtwith.com/cms/WordPress).

Where to Get Domains and Hosting

Often times if you register your domain and purchase hosting with the same company you will get a discount on one or the other.

For domain registration and hosting we recommend the following companies:

Hosting Company	Domain Registration (.com)	Hosting Price	Storage	Email Accounts	Our Rating
HostGator.com	$12.95 / Yr	$3.96 / Mo	Unlimited	Unlimited	4 / 5
GoDaddy.com	$14.99 / Yr	$3.49 / Mo	100 GB	100	2 / 5
1and1.com	$14.99 / Yr	$5.99 / Mo	100 GB	100	3.5 / 5
BlueHost.com	N/A	$3.95 / Mo	Unlimited	Unlimited	3 / 5

Prices subject to change.

Professional WordPress Website Themes

- ThemeForest.com – Truly amazing WordPress themes for as low as $15.Q

- TemplateMonster.com – Over 1,500 WordPress themes.

Social Networking Websites

These days you can't ignore the power of social networking websites like Facebook and Twitter. Odds are that you have an account with at least one of those two websites if not both and maybe several others such as Pinterest, LinkedIn, or Foursquare.

Having a website allows people to find you in search engines, but having a presence on social media sites lets you engage people where they "hang out" on the web. There are over 1.01 BILLION active monthly mobile users on Facebook.

Facebook and Twitter are a great way for you to keep your audience engaged and "in the know" about your app and brand. You can easily and quickly update people and get *immediate feedback*. In fact, if there is one benefit to getting involved in social media that we would put at #1:

It's customer service. There are certainly marketing advantages to having a social media presence; you can promote your app and encourage people to share information about it, but it is also a fantastic way for you to help out your customer base in an open and transparent environment.

Viral Content

Using social media sites as a way to keep your current audience informed is great, but it's also a great way to reach a new audience. And how do you do that? With viral content that encourages people to share. When people share content that you've produced it gets your name in front of more people. Sharing on social media sites is the new word-of-mouth marketing.

Content that has the potential to be shared over and over again is called *viral content* and two types of content that are most likely to be shared or "go viral" are images and videos. Particularly, images and video that are informative and/or entertaining.

Putting out images and videos about your app, or the niche that your app fits into, is a great way to provide useful or entertaining information to people, and information that is useful or entertaining tends to get shared.

An example of an image that you might post to your Facebook fans or Pinterest followers is an infographic. Infographics are graphical representations of data. Last year, we created an infographic for Dishpal which was picked up by the Huffington Post and received hundreds of social likes and shares.The infographic, titled, "10 of the World's Most Expensive Dishes," resulted in a massive download and brand awareness increase for the app.

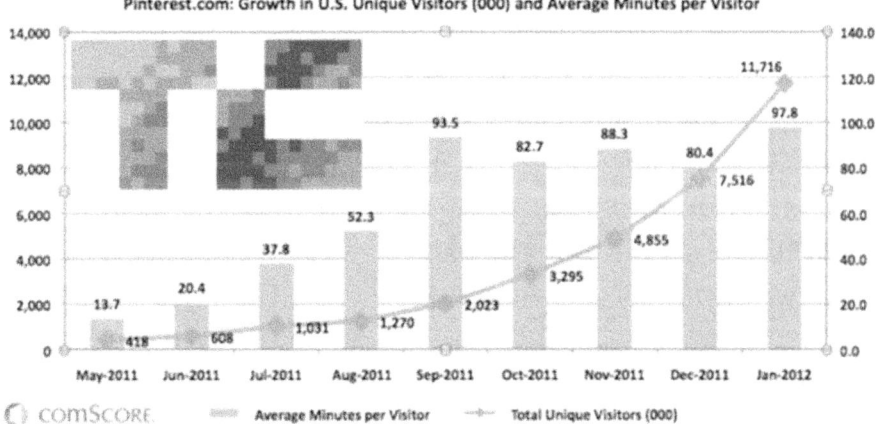

Pinterest.com: Growth in U.S. Unique Visitors (000) and Average Minutes per Visitor

comSCORE ▪▪▪ Average Minutes per Visitor —— Total Unique Visitors (000)

This infographic, though not working to the sell the app directly, provides useful information to people in a creative and memorable way, and since it is branded with the Dishpal name it positions them as somewhat of an authority on food knowledge.

The image sharing website Pinterest is one of the largest and fastest growing social media websites on the planet having surpassed 10 million users faster than any other website in history.

Posting a compelling infographic on Pinterest that "goes viral" could introduce your app and brand thousands of potential new customers.

SEO (Search Engine Optimization)

SEO, short for Search Engine Optimization, is the practice of optimizing your website so that it ranks well in search engines, thereby making it easier for people to find. There are two main areas involved with SEO.

On-Site SEO

On-site SEO is making sure that every page of your website is very relevant and well focused. If you have an app about song lyrics, then you don't want to talk a lot about guitar tabs on the same page. By ensuring that each of your pages are focused on a single topic – or KEYWORD - you make it easier for search engines to know what your pages are about and rank them accordingly. Successful on-site SEO means optimizing key elements of your web pages according to SEO best practices.

- **Meta Data** – This information is not typically seen by people, but gives search engines valuable information about your web pages. The most important meta tag, and one of the most important elements of your webpage overall for SEO, is the TITLE TAG. Make sure your TITLE TAG is descriptive and to-the point.

- **Headings** – Proper use of headings in your content clearly defines the importance of various sections. The importance of headings start at one and decrease in "power" from there. The two most common used headings are:

    ○ **H1** – Should be used only once per page and provide the over-arching theme.

    ○ **H2** – These are reserved for subheadings that provide supporting information about the **H1** tag.

- **Relevant & Unique Content** – The content on your web pages must be relevant to a single topic and be unique. Search engines value unique content.

Off-Site SEO

An important factor used by search engines in determining how to rank a site is how many back links there are pointing to the site. Back links are exactly what they sound like: links from one site pointing back to another. Search engines view back links like votes. The more "votes" you have for your site, the more important a search engine considers your site to be.

These concepts about SEO are merely a high level overview. You can learn more about SEO directly from Google with their Search Engine Optimization Starter's Guide.

Getting the Media's Attention

You can't just dump your app in the marketplace and expect it to get downloads. You have to get the word out. One very effective way of doing this is by executing a successful PR campaign.

Getting your app covered by an established website or news source is a great way to get word out about the launch of your app to the masses. Press coverage of your app also provides a lot of SEO value to your website if your press release or an article about your app has links in it.

Who to Reach Out To

There a lot of websites and news organizations that you should try to get your press release to no matter what your app is, but you should also target websites that are specific to your app's niche. If your app is a game, then send press releases to gaming websites. If your app is a photography tool, then send press releases out to photography and digital imaging related websites.

Some of the best places you could hope to get coverage regardless of what your app does are:
- Mashable
- GIZMODO
- TechCrunch
- Huffington Post
- New York Times

Press Releases

Press releases provide many benefits to your business. They are great for SEO and can quickly get news of your app out to hundreds or thousands of people. Many websites across many genres routinely pick up press releases and re-post them to their audiences automatically. You may post a single press release, but it may get re-printed thousands of times!

Ideally, you want your press release to get picked up by a major news website such as those mentioned above. In this case you should submit your press release directly to their editorial departments. This can be tricky; as such contact information is not always easy to come by. While many press release distribution services offer free distribution to small websites, to get your press release on the desk of major influencers in your niche you'll need to pay a premium fee, but this can be well worth it. Having your app covered on a top website like Mashable could launch your download numbers into the stratosphere.

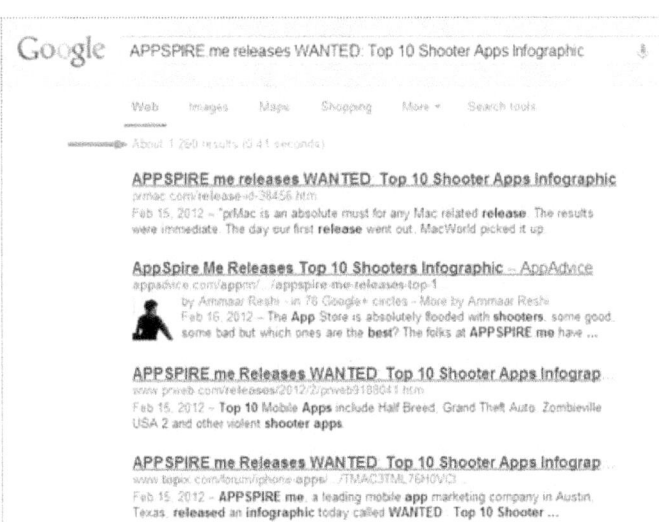

In this Google search result you can see a press release from APPSPIRE.me picked up and reprinted over a thousand times.

A few of the more popular press release distribution services are:

- APPSPIRE.me (specializing in mobile app marketing, of course!)
- PRWeb
- PRLog
- PR Newswire
- PRMac

Getting App Reviews

Reviews can make or break your app in a couple of ways. First, the obvious: having a lot of good reviews encourages people that your app is worth their time and money to download. There are thousands upon thousands of apps in the two major app markets, so making sure your app has a good reputation there is a must.

But the second reason isn't so obvious. There are many other places outside of the major app markets where your app can get reviewed that can drive additional downloads, sales and provide more visibility in search engines. You can contact these websites directly, give them a free copy of your app, and hope they will review it. In many cases you can negotiate for premium options for a fee such as being featured on their home page, inclusion in newsletters or social media mentions, for example.

A few app review websites are:

- TheDailyAppShow
- CraveOnline
- AppAdvice

YouTube has become rich with all kinds of reviews including app reviews. Video reviews allow for people to show specific examples of exactly how your app functions. There are entire YouTube channels with millions of views dedicated entirely to reviewing and demonstrating mobile apps, such as:

- Crazy Mike's Apps
- AppVee
- Mobile Burn

Coverage on these well-trafficked review sites will get your app plenty of exposure to a much targeted market: people interested in mobile apps. Crazy Mike's Apps YouTube channel currently has over 12,000 subscribers; AppVee over 33,000, and MobileBurn over 55,000.

Pre-Press Launch

One way to get covered by a high-traffic website is to offer them a pre-press opportunity. This means that you handpick a few websites and give them a beta version of your app before you officially launch it. Blogs and websites love to get exclusive content. You will find that most webmasters are eager to cover your app if they are getting their hands on it before anyone else.

Again, you should target your pre-press launch efforts to your app's specific niche and broader topic websites like app and tech news websites.

Staying in the Media's Attention

To yield the best results over the long haul it is important that you keep at it. Any time you have a major update to your app you should put out a new press release. There are tons of app review websites and YouTube channels and there are always more popping up, so getting reviews should be an ongoing process.

You can also leverage the pre-press launch strategy with future updates to your existing app, especially if the update comes with major changes and/or fixes.

In-App Advertising Campaigns

If you've got a mobile app that you want to advertise, you're in luck. In-app advertising is hands down the best form of advertising we have ever seen. Whereas traditional advertisements like print, billboards and even web ads can't produce direct results, in-app advertising does. The best type of in-app advertising for apps today is CPI, or Cost Per Install.

Cost Per Install means that you don't pay a cent until someone actually downloads your app. There is not a single form of advertising that is as effective as CPI, regardless of what your business is. PPC (Pay Per Click) ads charge you per web banner click and may send someone to your website, but they still may not buy anything. In fact, you can spend thousands of dollars on a PPC campaign and not make a single penny. CPI, however, guarantees that your app gets downloaded or you don't pay anything. On top of this, the more downloads you get, the higher your app rises in the iTunes or Google Play Store, so CPI advertising is a win-win situation.

Ad networks

The first thing you'll discover about CPI advertising is that there is a smorgasbord of ad networks available to choose from. Some are highly effective at keeping your CPI costs low. Other ad networks can reach your exact target audience. Finding the right ad network for your app can take a few phone calls, emails, and some research, but it's an imperative step so don't rush through it.

One of the most popular ad networks today is Facebook App Installs. This network has a huge list of demographics to choose from to find your target audience. However, the options can be a bit overwhelming, and without prior experience on running these types of ads you're likely to spend much more on CPI than you expected. Your best bet is to have an experienced advertising firm like APPSPIRE.me run the ads for you. You'll have to pay an extra fee of course, but ultimately the results will be much better and it will save you money in the long run.

Types of ads

Ads come in three different forms: static, dynamic, and video. Static ads are a single image that does not change or move. Dynamic ads are multiple static images that rotate. Video ads actually display a video that can play automatically or after the user hits a play button. The more dynamic an ad is, the more it costs and the more loyal user base it connects with. If a user is willing to watch an entire video before they download your app, they are obviously your prime customer. Social media apps need video ad campaigns because their app is based on users using it frequently and spreading the word to others. Game apps or Utility apps just need to be downloaded once, so a static or dynamic ad is usually suitable. Your app category will weigh heavily on the type of ad network you choose.

Knowing your competition

Even if your app is the best of the best, designed flawlessly and perfectly suited for its audience, the competition will gauge how expensive your ad campaign will be. For instance, gaming apps are flooded with competition. There are so many game apps available that getting to the top 10 of your subcategory can sometimes be costly. This is because not only is there a lot of competition, but your competitors are spending thousands and thousands of dollars per day on ad campaigns to stay up in the rankings. If one app spends 10k per day to stay in the top ten, the next app has to spend more than that to stay in the top 10. It's a like a game of king of the mountain; every app is spending more and more on ads per day to get to the top.

However, if your app has little competition, like a gaming app for girls, your ad costs can be extremely low. One of our former clients, an app called Princessy Cupcakes, was able to break into the top 10 of her category twice with a budget less than 3k. This is because at the time games-for-girls genre was a relatively untapped genre, and her CPI costs came to be very cost efficient.

Do some research on your competition before launching an ad campaign so you can gauge your budget. Talking with ad networks, finding out what apps are in the top 10 of your app category and how many downloads they are getting are good ways to start doing this.

Download costs vs. Ranking and Organic vs. Paid Downloads

Ad networks promise downloads, but not ranking increase. However, your app will rise in rankings with downloads naturally. The reason that you should be more concerned about ranking increase rather than downloads is that once your ad budget runs out, the downloads will typically start to slow down. However, if you break in to the top 10 of your store category, users will discover and download your app through search, not ads, which mean you don't have to pay for the download. The higher in rankings your app is, the better the chance that it will get organic downloads, not paid. That's the secret to keeping your CPI costs down, focus on rankings, not downloads.

SRO (Store Review Optimization)

If you have an app that is already live, or you are about to launch one, more than likely you have store reviews on your mind. How to get them, how to avoid negative reviews, and so forth should be things that you are thinking about whether your app is live or soon to be live in iTunes and/or Google Play. Getting reviews is relatively easy, making sure that they are positive reviews takes a little bit of work.

But before we jump into SRO (Store Review Optimization), let's be clear about what store reviews can and can't do. App reviews are a powerful asset for your app, but they are not a necessary device to stay in the top rankings of iTunes or Google Play. Both iTunes and Google Play store rankings are denoted by downloads per day, not reviews.

Also, it is better to have a few negative reviews of your app than no reviews at all. No reviews suggest that no one is taking interest in your app, and the psychology sends a deterrent signal to possible customers. Negative reviews are almost unavoidable: there's always that one person who has something bad to say no matter what. What you should be worried about more than receiving negative reviews, is concentrating on positive reviews and learning from the negative reviews.

How to get positive reviews

If your app functions well, serves a purpose and has an audience, and has an attractive design, there is no reason why it shouldn't receive positive reviews. The trick is finding the audience to review it. The first thing most app owners do is ask their friends, peers, and family to download the app and review it. While this is a good first step, most friend reviews are pretty transparent and say things like, "This app is perfect!" and leave 5 stars.

While this practice is expected, most downloaders are aware of it and wary if friend reviews are all that exists. What your app will need to balance out these friend reviews is reviews from real downloaders – complete strangers to the owners of the app. We suggest three methods for obtaining real reviews:

1. Submit to Review Sites.
2. Send out a Press Release.
3. Social Media Engagement.

Submit to Review Sites

There are hundreds of app reviews sites tailored for every kind of app on any platform. You can do a Google search to find a review site that fits your app and submit your app for review. Bear in mind that online review sites do not translate directly to app store reviews, but if the site gets a decent amount of traffic others will download your app and review it.

Send out a Press Release

Press releases, if done correctly, will get picked up by hundreds of sites and start generating immediate reviews for your app. You can try sending one out on your own through PRWeb or some other PR service agency, but we suggest you leave this to a professional and have an app PR agency like APPSPIRE.me do it for you.

Social Media Engagement

Social Media is one of the most powerful tools to garner interaction for you app. Starting a Facebook Page, Twitter Page, YouTube, Google+ or any other social media site and creating a compelling social media campaign will get an audience focused on your app and start generating reviews.

Turning a Negative into a Positive

If you receive one or more negative reviews in the app store for your app, do not fret. Use this as a method to improve your app, engage your audience, and garner attention. For instance, if you receive a negative review that points out a bug in the app, fix the bug and promote that you fixed it. If the review states something like "crashes every time I launch the app offline," fix the bug in an updated version, and announce that you have fixed it in the app's description, social media pages, and any other active mediums you may have. This shows your audience that you are listening to their voice, are attentive to their needs, and that your app is not fly-by-night, but is here to stay. You may want to even go as far as thanking the reviewer for pointing out the problem on your social media pages, and announcing that you have fixed it. If potential downloaders are going so far as to read your reviews, then more than likely they have read your app description where you addressed the negative reviews and fixed the problem.

Creative Link Bait

Link bait is content that is so incredibly awesome that it encourages people to link to it and share it. Content like this has great benefits for SEO (Search Engine Optimization) since it can exponentially grow back links to your app's website, but it also works wonders for branding and name recognition. When you publish and distribute a piece of well crafted link bait with your name on it that gets shared a lot, or "goes viral" then you've managed to introduce your name to hundreds, or even thousands of people.

But link bait, no matter how good it might be, doesn't go viral on its own. You have to give it a bit of a push. Not only should you publish link bait on your own web properties but you should get it out to as many other people, blogs and social networking websites as possible to help it.

Typically, link bait must be of superb quality do any good. Link bait that looks amateurish not only makes your brand look amateurish but it is unlikely to get picked up. If you are keen on creating your own link bait don't cut corners and rush it. If you don't have the necessary skills to produce link bait on your own it is highly recommended that you hire a professional. There are many places that specialize in the production of various types of link bait.

So...what exactly does link bait look like?

Infographics

Infographics present data in an interesting and graphical way. Creating infographics around your apps theme is a great way to inform the public about your app, its subject matter, and the problem it solves. Memorable, eye-catching infographics are easily shared and get great traction on social media sites.

A few examples of good infographics:
- Best iPhone Apps for Halloween
- What Home Cooks are Grilling
- A World Without Google

Memes

If you are at all active on Facebook then you've probably are already familiar with what a meme is. In a nutshell, a meme is a photo with a catch phrase in text posted on it. Memes can go viral very quickly on account of their simplicity. This simplicity, however, also makes their staying power relatively short lived.

Regardless, memes are very effective creative link baits for your app. The trick to harnessing a meme's power is have a meme that is funny, catchy, related to your app, and has all the necessary contact info on it to link back to your app. You can put a small footer in the meme that simply says, "Brought to you by (name of your app)" and place a QR code next to it that links to your website or download page. Website links can be tracked, whereas download pages cannot. The choice is up to you.

Where the real ingenuity of a meme comes in is your team's creative brainstorming. You must, above all, have a meme idea that can go viral, which you can try to think up on your own or hire a team (like APPSPIRE.me) to do so. After the meme is created, push it out through press releases or social media sites, and track downloads to measure its success.

BuzzFeed

If you spend any time on Facebook, then you've certainly come across a link to a BuzzFeed article. BuzzFeed is a social and entertainment-based news site, with daily articles uploaded that promote social activity. BuzzFeed is known for publishing lists and quizzes that quickly go viral if they get featured on the homepage. The nice thing about BuzzFeed is that it lets anyone set up an account and post their own quiz or article. However, the homepage contest is curated by the staff, so unless you have an inside connection, your article will likely not get much traction without some advertising and marketing help. APPSPIRE.me has been fortunate enough to have many of our clients featured on the BuzzFeed homepage, which resulted in massive growth in social media awareness, fans, and ultimately, downloads.

List and Quiz Sites

Ever since the popularity of BuzzFeed took off, there have been dozens of list and quiz sites that popped up in BuzzFeed's wake. Many of these sites do the exact same thing as BuzzFeed, but they don't have the social fan base that BuzzFeed has, so their efforts aren't quit as effective. If you decide to use one of these external sites, be prepared to back it up with a healthy marketing and advertising campaign or else your efforts will not be fruitful.

White Papers

White papers are professional reports on a subject, or many times just part of a subject, that are freely distributed. White papers typically propose a solution to a common problem in a given niche. The long term benefit to giving away white paper is that, like with infographics, it gets your name out on the web in a simple and shareable way. You can syndicate white papers on article directories and document sharing websites like DocStoc and Scribd.

You can also offer your white papers on your own website in exchange for a visitor's email address. This is a great way to build your email address list. White papers should be well-researched and packed with solid information.

A few possible examples of white paper topics for a few apps:

TYPE OF APP	WHITE PAPER TITLE
Calorie counter for dieters	How to Avoid Gaining Extra Holiday Pounds
Photography effects & filters	Framing the Perfect Portrait for Beginners
A word puzzle game	Finish the New York Times Crossword Fast!

Comic Strips

Short comic strips are a particularly great way to promote games and novelty apps. The concept is similar to infographics except that you're primary purpose is to demonstrate something instead of simply showing data. In order to really go viral across the web your comic strip should be funny!

You can think of comic strips as graphical, funny white papers. They present a problem and offer a solution in an amusing way.

Videos

Videos are the most popular form of media on the web simply because of all the information they are able to pack into a small package. Funny, amusing, moving, inspirational; videos can create and capture these emotions much more fully than images or text alone. And consider this little statistic: YouTube is the SECOND LARGEST SEARCH ENGINE behind Google.

You Tube™ USAGE STATS

• More than 1 billion unique users visit YouTube each month

• Over 6 billion hours of video are watched each month on YouTube—that's almost an hour for every person on Earth

• 100 hours of video are uploaded to YouTube every minute

Not only do videos make for great viral content, but they can be incredibly useful in instructing people on how to use your app as well. These types of videos are called "explainer videos" or "app trailers" and they are extremely valuable for apps that require some know-how to be used to their fullest potential.

A few explainer videos by How It Works Media:
- Appoconomy
- Proclivity Systems
- Starmap Astronomy

QR Codes

Believe it or not, not all forms of link bait have to be digital, thanks to a little thing called QR codes. You have likely seen these things around in magazines, on posters, business cards, and websites. QR codes look like nothing more than a jumble of black squares, but they actually hold information in much the same was a typical bar code. Scan these QR codes with your smartphone to see how they work:

URL	Phone Number	Text

With a QR code you can make physical objects linkable in a way. When scanned with a smartphone, a QR code can do all sorts of useful things. It can automatically direct someone to a website, open and pre-populate an email, share a link to Facebook, or send someone directly to your app's download page in the iPhone or Android app markets.

QR codes allow you to extend your app's reach into the real world. Does your app recommend great roadside stops for travelers? Then print up some posters about your app with a QR code linking to your download page or website and distribute them to local travel agencies, RV dealerships, and hotels.

Making QR codes is extremely easy thanks to automated QR code generators like these:

- Kaywa QR Code
- GoQR.com
- QR Stuff

Social Media Campaigns

Social media campaigns are a great way to build buzz about your app and encourage people to spread awareness through social sharing. Social media campaigns are usually built around a contest that lets users engage with your brand in a fun and memorable way.

While a social media campaign can be successful and grow on its own if you put in a lot of work marketing it, you will mostly likely get the best results if you also run an advertising campaign in conjunction with it.

Facebook Contests and Ads

 There are currently over 500 million people on Facebook, so if there's one place you definitely want to run a social media campaign it's there. Typically, a Facebook campaign is done to increase the number of LIKES on your Facebook page. While you can certainly run a campaign just to get people to download your app, you should try to work in a component that requires them to LIKE your page as well. This way they become somewhat of a "captive audience" that you can market to with future campaigns.

Running little contests on Facebook can be incredibly simple, but you must abide by Facebook's promotions guidelines. While you can certainly do something as simple as posting "First ten people to comment on the post will get a FREE download of our new app!" this is actually a violation of Facebook's terms and conditions. Officially, Facebook contests and campaigns must be run using a 3rd party application.

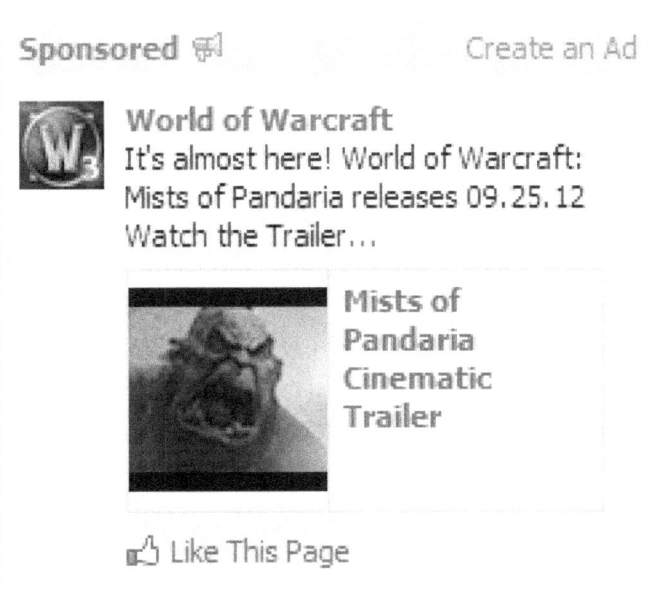

To learn more about Facebook's contest and promotion guidelines here:

https://www.facebook.com/page_guidelines.php

In addition to, or independently of, your Facebook social media campaign you can also run extremely effective Facebook ads. Because Facebook collects so much data about people, their advertising platform allows for incredibly precise demographic targeting. You can not only target ads based on gender, age, and location but also on a virtually endless amount of very specific interests. If you want people to download your guitar tuner application you can target your Facebook ads to people who are interested in guitars, Eddie Van Halen, home recording, songwriting, or any number of related interests.

Facebook's advertising is a PPC (Pay Per Click) model, which means that each time someone clicks on your add you will be charged a small fee. Because of this, it is very important that you target your ads precisely. Otherwise you may pay for a lot of clicks that don't result in downloads of your app or LIKES to your Facebook page.

Staying Active on Twitter

Twitter is the place to be for RIGHT NOW , real-time news and information and this is where you should be putting out your RIGHT NOW news and information about your app and social media campaigns.

There are two primary keys to making Twitter work for you:

1. Frequency – Twitter is a fast paced environment. Tweets are fleeting, so you improve the chances of your tweets being seen by tweeting often. Tweet all the time about everything! Obviously you want to tweet about your app, but also tweet often about the niche your app serves. Is your app a resource for vegetarian dining? Then tweet about your favorite restaurants and vegetarian stores.

2. Hashtags – Hashtags help your tweets get found in Twitter search and indexed & categorized by other websites such as Google. For instance, to help you get found on Twitter for the word "vegetarian" you would use the hashtag #vegetarian. "This is my favorite #vegetarian restaurant!"

YouTube Advertising

As mentioned in the chapter *Creative Link Bait*, YouTube is the second largest search engine after Google. Additionally, videos are the most sought after forms of media when people go online. So it goes without saying that you should have videos about your app on YouTube. But YouTube also offers another tool and this advertising.

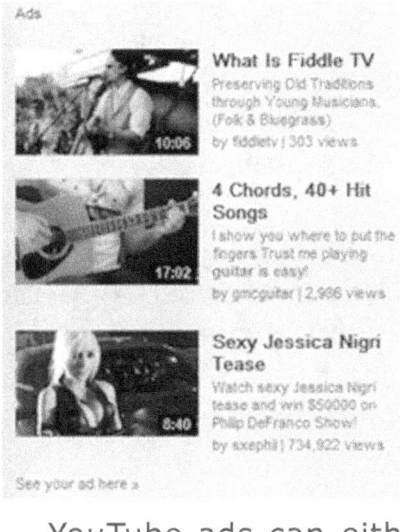

YouTube videos promoted as ads.

Similar to Facebook, you can target your YouTube ads based on interest, or more specifically, video content. If you want to get people to your guitar tuner app's website you could have ads about your app show up in, or next to, videos featuring people playing guitar.

YouTube ads can either be a simple message that appears at the bottom of other user's videos, or a short video that plays before another user's video. You can also opt to promote your own videos, which means that they will show up at the top of YouTube search results pages for searches on keywords related to your app.

To learn more about YouTube's advertising options you can visit this URL:

http://www.youtube.com/yt/advertise/index.html

Live Events

Live Events are a great way to get your app exposure to a large group of people quickly. You no doubt live in or near a major city where there are often sizeable events going on such as music festivals, marathons, conferences, parades, and carnivals.

Attaching your app's or brand's name to a well-known and well-loved live event is a fantastic way to introduce it to an audience in a way that will stand out in their minds. And if you do it in a clever and engaging way you're sure to gain many new customers.

Sponsorships

Events, big or small, don't pay for themselves. They are funded by sponsors. Putting up some money to sponsor an event gets your name attached to it and promoted alongside it. You've likely seen large print ads and billboards promoting a large event in your city that mentions all or some of the companies that contributed to make that event possible.

By sponsoring a well-established event that is popular you are aligning your brand with something that people already have a positive view of in their minds.

While sponsorships can get expensive – you probably won't end up on a billboard or mentioned on the radio for an event unless you pay a premium – events typically have several sponsorship options covering many price ranges. You may be able to pay a smaller fee to just have your name put on a newspaper advertisement, or you may get to have your name a banner at the event.

Although there's no limit to the type of event you can cover, you should definitely put events that are closely related to your app at the top of the list. If your app is a music related app, you should sponsor a big music event like Vans Warped tour. If your app is a social sharing app, sponsor tech related conferences like SXSW.

Video Coverage

Don't stop at sponsoring the event. Take part in the event and broadcast it. No matter how big and popular the event is there will always people who can't make it there who wish they could. You can bring the event to them by broadcasting it on your website, Facebook, YouTube, and Ustream.

Ustream is an ideal scenario for this because it allows you to broadcast live as the event is happening, instead of taping and then uploading later to your website. You can set up a Ustream account and promote the fact that you'll be broadcasting from the event. This will allow you to reach people worldwide.

Your Own Event

If there are no sponsorship options that fit within your budget, you might look at putting on your own event. While this may sound like a MORE expensive option, it doesn't have to be. In fact, once you become the organizer you can actually have people paying you to sponsor of your event.

In many cases you can piggyback your event off of a larger event going on at the same time. During by South by Southwest (SXSW) in Austin, Texas – one of the largest music and media conferences in the world – you'll find many "Unofficial SXSW" events going on at the same time. Passes to the event can be expensive so there are always people looking out for free options, either because they couldn't afford tickets to the actual event, or because they blew all their money on the event.

Branding at Events

Whether you sponsor an event or host your own it is important that you properly brand the event with your app's or app company's name. Put your name on everything. If you're throwing a small concert featuring local musicians hang a giant banner on the stage with your app or company name on it. If you're sponsoring a BBQ cook off have napkins printed up with your app name on them.

Staying Successful

Once you do an initial campaign boost, whether it's based around a launch or update, your downloads, rankings, and media presence may start to drop after the buzz has died down. If you want a longterm successful app, you need to include further marketing and advertising procedures to make sure your app continues onward and upward. Your app's long term success is completely dependent on your marketing and advertising efforts, both of which are ongoing business tactics. The more money you invest in marketing and advertising, the more successful your app will be in the short and long term.

Updates to your App

Every app should get updated at least every few months to stay relevant.

These updates can include:

- Bug fixes,
- New features,
- Redesigns.

If you're not sure what you should update your app with, read the user reviews and look for complaints or compliments. These can be helpful hints on what your customers are looking for, and what you can do to satisfy them further and build some buzz around your app. Once your updates have been made, be sure to mention it in your app store description.

Creative Link Bait

Creative link bait, like infographics or interactive media, are great methods for keeping your app relevant. Task your creative team with creating a series of creative link baits that are all tied together and will all encourage downloads for your app. You can launch these daily, weekly, bi-weekly, or monthly, but the more often the better.

Ad Campaigns

If you've followed the instructions in this book thus far, then you've already had at least one successful ad campaign. Though you may feel you've hit the mark and are content with just one, you'll need to do more to stay on top. Most of our successful customers don't contact us for a few months after their first campaign has ended, but once the buzz has died down from that, they come back for another boost.

If you don't have the budget for a continuous ad campaign, one campaign every few months will suffice. Depending on your app category and the app market at the time, you may need to spend $5,000-$10,000 every few months to stay on top. If the ad campaign is run correctly, it will encourage organic downloads and turn into profit. If it isn't run correctly, the ads will simply be money spent and not encourage growth.

Social Media Campaigns

Social media is an incredibly useful tool that is cost effective and can be used on an ongoing basis. If you have a creative social media team, task them with inventing new ideas on social media contests, games, and other tactics to increase your social media fan base and interaction. You can also do Facebook and YouTube advertising on your campaigns to spread the word. Above all, keep in mind that the end efforts of your social media campaign is to drive users to download and use your app, not just hang around your social media page.

PR Efforts

Its important to stay in the media's attention, but sending out random press releases with no real news will quickly turn your PR efforts into spam. Don't send out a press release without a reason - give the media something to work with. Any updates to your app are good content for a press release. Also, if your app has recently hit a new milestone, such as breaking into the top 10 or 5 of its app category, let the media know if it's new found success.

It is in your app's best interest to send out a press release at least every two months about it. If you don't have any news to report, make some. Update your app, start a social media contest, create or join a live event involving your app, create and launch a creative link bait campaign. There are dozens of things you can do for your app to make it stay relevant in the media.

About the Authors

Carson Barker is the owner and founder of APPSPIRE.me, a leading mobile app marketing agency. He has been working in marketing for over 7 years, and has created and executed dozens of successful online and real world marketing campaigns for business such as The Associated Press, Open Labs, FramesDirect.com, and many more.

Carson holds a bachelor's degree in journalism from St. Edwards University and is currently seeking his Master's degree in writing. Prior to establishing *APPSPIRE.me* as one of the most successful app marketing agencies, Carson was a journalist, writing for The Austin Chronicle, The Austin-American Statesman, People Magazine, and other popular websites and magazines. He currently lives and works in Austin, Texas.

Clif Haley is a serial entrepreneur, having dabbled in and profited from a myriad of endeavors both online and off. He's been an Internet Marketing professional for over 9 years specializing in Search Engine Optimization. During his tenure with ClickResponse.net Clif helped many small businesses grow their website traffic by increasing their organic search rankings. He is currently SEO Director for Dreamstime.com, a world leader in stock photography since 2000.

Clif co-founded the Internet Marketing firm Space Chimp Media and Mobile App Marketing firm *APPSPIRE.me* with Carson Barker. Clif has been a published humorist for The Austin-American Statesman newspaper. He resides in Waldron, Arkansas and regularly supplements his income by selling custom designs on CafePress, providing voiceovers, consulting, and freelancing.

www.ingramcontent.com/pod-product-compliance
Lightning Source LLC
Chambersburg PA
CBHW051251170526
45165CB00004B/1660